The little gr
of dancing...

Rueda!

*...or "Rueda Makes
The World Go Around!"*

Daniel Allen

ISBN: 1497314003
ISBN–13: 978-1497314009

Dedicated to Tanya

With many thanks to Anita, Ariana, Coco, Cristina, Dae, Doris, Fraudy, Gabriela, Graeme, James, Jenny, Joe, Juan, Karol, Laurie, Lilly, Louisa, Marc, Marieke, Max, Mellissa, Moro, Nikoletta, Rafael, Rebecca, Rie, Suyen, Trung, Valery, Yarima and anyone else who has helped, influenced, taught or danced with me over all these years…

Facebook: https://www.facebook.com/DanAllenBooks

CONTENTS

Part I: La Rueda

1	What is Rueda?	3
2	Rueda de Casino	7
3	Some Fun Facts About Rueda	11
4	Rueda and Social Dancing	13
5	Group Vs. Self	15
6	Los Básicos	17
7	Arriba, Abajo, Al Centro… Guapea!	21
8	A Quick Tip For The Partner Leader	23
9	'El Cantante'	25

Part II: Las Figuras

10	Moves From Guapea	33
11	The Enchufla Family	41
12	Slightly More Complicated Guapea Moves	49
13	Al Centro Moves	53
14	Turn The Wheel Inside Out	57

Part III: On Your Own

15 Your Call!   61

16 Create Your Own Moves   67

17 Fun With Rueda   69

18 Rueda de Bachata   73

19 Afterword...   75

20 More Resources   77

Part I:
La Rueda

What is Rueda?

'Rueda' (or 'Rueda de Casino') is a circular social or folk group dance that involves one person calling a move and everyone completing it at the same time. The name 'Rueda' in Spanish literally means a "wheel". Rueda de Casino is its formal name from the fact that the dance used to be danced in the large casino halls in Cuba, but it is most commonly simply referred to as Rueda. I like to think of it as 'salsa in a circle', with one leader, many sub-leaders and possibly even many more followers (you can do Rueda with two followers – 'Rueda Con Dos Mujeres').

To experience Rueda is unlike any other salsa partner dancing – whether it is LA, NY or Cuban style. Rueda is a group (I like to think of it as a community) of dancers that must listen and interact with patience, humour and a willingness to have fun with all the unexpected surprises – both new or crazy moves, and with the mistakes that people make. It is not a dance in which one goes to show off their latest solo moves. However, there is plenty of room for individual flair and expression, as long as it fits into the overall timing of the called moves.

I was attracted to Rueda in the beginning when I was learning salsa, as I didn't need to think of what to do – someone else was calling all the moves for a change! I could relax and enjoy dancing, maybe even say 'hi' to all the ladies, relax and watch all the fun while someone else decided what to do and when... all I had to do was listen for the call and do it (if I knew the move!). However, I soon felt the pressure to begin calling, as it is nice when there are many different callers as everyone has their own style and moves they like to do best. I forced myself to leave the comfort and safety of my carefree, 'responsible-less' position and join the ranks of callers.

I instantly became addicted to calling. I found the challenge of deciding what moves were best to do with the average level of experience of most of the dancers, and trying to make my moves match the music, plus keep everyone interested and having fun, was exhilarating. I would go home, make lists of possible moves and combinations, imagining them with certain songs. At the same time though, I also began to gently 'volunteer' others to call and encourage them, just to get them started feeling comfortable and confident. I loved how differently everyone called, some fast, some slow, some crazy – and learning what their favourite moves were. I learnt as much watching them as they might have learnt from my 'mentoring' them. I soon fell back in love with just being a 'follower' and doing what everyone else told me to. That's one of the wonderful things about Rueda – you can call the shots, or just relax and enjoy not having to think at all (...well, not very much!). Whatever you do, the most important thing to do is to smile, say 'hi' to your neighbor, and have fun!

Rueda de Casino

Rueda evolved from the Gavotte, Quadrille and Contredanse social folk dances from the U.K. and Europe that made their way to Cuba through the Spanish, English and French influences. The Gavotte was a circular dance holding hands, while the Quadrille was danced in a square with four couples facing each other, and involved a 'forward and backward' movement (much like the basic Rueda move 'Guapea'). The 'head' couple would first dance a move, and then the other three couples would repeat the same move. The Cubans began to create more of a circle of couples dancing, and eventually incorporating some more simple interaction between the dancers (like 'Pa mi, pa it' – a version of the children's "Pat-a-cake" game), followed by beginning to swap partners by having everyone doing the same move at the same time. Then, all you had to do was add in some 'accents and flavouring' from the African heritage of many Cubans, and you end up with Rueda de Casino!

I have danced swing, ceroc, salsa, rueda, bachata, forró, zouk and many other partner social dances, and I find it interesting when people try to trace the 'roots' or origins of a dance or music style. Sometimes, I think to myself, "you know there are only so many ways you can turn a partner dancing - left or right!" In addition, if you are dancing in any organised group, there are only so many ways you can do it: circles, squares or lines (yes, you can dance Rueda in a line too – it's called 'Rueda Linea'). So most partner social dancing (such as folk dancing) has much more in common than not. I see Rueda as simply a local geographical and cultural variation on the many group folk dances from the U.K., Europe, Latin America and Africa.

Some of the earliest Rueda moves were the simplest ones:

Vamos arriba/abajo – walking forward or backward in a circle

Pa' mi, pa' ti – similar to the kid's game 'pat-a-cake' where each partner claps hands against the person next to them

Paseo – leading your partner in a circle around you with one hand

Lazo – similar to the 'Paseo' but with more turning involved

Cadena – turning the partner of the couple next to you around and back (while someone else turned your partner)

Ocho – making a circle around the partner next to you before returning to your partner

Vueltas – each partner does a simple turn while stepping in towards the centre of the circle (sometimes also as a couple)

Puente – a rather more complicated move where the men build a "bridge" with their arms interlocked in the centre and the women pas underneath and then back out again from under the bridge, before changing partners

So you can see, Rueda started with fairly simple, easy, fun moves, and in my opinion, is sometimes the best way to dance Rueda so everyone can enjoy it and have fun!

Some Fun Facts About Rueda

Sometimes a male caller will see a woman he likes in the circle and he will call quick moves to get her next to him, so that he can then call something he wants to do like a 'Besito' (a kiss) ...or a female caller could do the same if she sees a male she likes!

Women do not traditionally call Rueda, but it is becoming more common, either while following, or as a woman leading.

Rueda is a historically a simple folk dance, but it can sometimes be used as a competitive contest of complicated moves to find the best male dancer - if a man makes a mistake or doesn't know a call, he (and his partner) step out of the circle and the last man standing is the best dancer.

Some Rueda calls are not even real words, nor grammatically correct, but if you know Spanish, the names are lovely and often have a hidden, kind of 'tongue-in-cheek' humour.

For example, in Rueda we have three moves that are grouped together. The first is, 'La Prima' = "the cousin". Second is, 'La Hermana' = "the sister", and if you dance those two moves plus add a third, it becomes 'La Familia' = "the family".

In addition, I like the fact that we have the one name for the move 'La Familia', whereas in LA Style, it would be called something like a "reverse cross-body lead, under-arm spin, 360-degree turn exchange!"

Most Rueda names are just baseball terms, numbers, objects (that vaguely represent the shape of the move, for example: 'Sombrero' and 'Montaña'), or names of family, places or women's names, plus many other various silly things like drinks, such as 'Coca Cola'.

If you are dancing Rueda in a loud club, or with such a large group that it is hard to hear the calls, there are hand signals for some of the moves. For instance, 'Sombrero' is signalled by tapping on your head like putting on a hat. 'Montaña' is moving your hand up and down like a wave indicating the rolling hills and valleys of the mountains. There are a few other signals, but sadly, not enough to be able to call each Rueda move (there are literally hundreds of Rueda moves and variations!) so sometimes what we do instead is 'echo' call – once a caller has called a move on 1 beat, one or two other people evenly spaced around the circle will immediately echo the same call on beat 2 or 3 so that everyone can hear it.

Rueda and Social Dancing

It is possible to dance Rueda in a club social dancing, however it is often hard to hear the caller. As mentioned, there are hand signals for some more common moves, but it is more often a problem for people who have not danced Rueda together, as many schools teach different moves, sometimes using different names, and quite often either changing or not after certain moves. For example, most will do a 'Dile Que No' after an 'Ochenta', but then some will also automatically do a 'Dame' after that as well, so it is best to keep your eyes on the caller for a hint what to do.

Often you can tell a Rueda dancer at a social dance, as he will lead individual moves followed by a 'Dile Que No' in-between each move. It is a habit Rueda dancers get into and can sometimes become a part of their social dancing style. The good thing about Rueda compared to social dancing is that you don't really have to ask a partner to dance, and if you do, it is a lot less stressful as you both know that you are really only asking her to join the circle with you and do the first move or two, and then change partners. Even if you can't find a partner to join the circle with, just get in between two couples and you will pick up a partner on the next move... If there are quite a few 'partner-less' people in the circle, pick a spot that is not next to any one of them, so that you are staggered evenly throughout the circle and not all in a bunch next to each other.

Just like social dancing, personal hygiene is very important in Rueda – maybe even more important; you are going to be dancing with many partners at once, who all have to smell, feel and touch you! It should be obvious, but always practice good hygiene and wear deodorant, use mouthwash, etc. Also, make sure your nails are clipped and/or filed smooth. If necessary, bring an extra shirt or two if you sweat a lot. Men and women should both wear comfortable, flat, soft street shoes – not work shoes with big heavy hard soles, or high-heels. Women should also wear tops that do not have any loose attachments like a shawl, etc. that can get tangled in their partner's arms.

Group Vs. Self

How to make the transition from Calling the Shots to Being Told What to do!

There is more than one way to have fun with Rueda – obviously dancing in a group with great people all in unison is nice... but what if you want to break out and improvise or express yourself a little?

A good friend of mine said to me once that his first Rueda teacher told him, "Just start when you're supposed to, and finish when you're supposed to, and who cares what you do in between!" I'm probably paraphrasing this third-hand advice, but the point is – have fun doing whatever you do in Rueda! If someone calls an 'Enchufla' and you want to add a little spice, do it! I personally, add a little kind of slide-back step either at the end (6-7) of an 'Enchufla', or a 'La Prima', as I go under her arm. It's not going to stand out and cause any distractions or problems for the group (unless you are in a choreo competition) but your partner will probably notice and smile.

Now, I know I am contradicting the rule that if a beginner doesn't know a move, they should just smile at their partner and tell them they don't know it and continue doing 'Guapea' (or 'Al Centro') until it is time to change partners... but if you are a more advanced beginning dancer, you can improvise. Most 'complicado' moves are going to be 16-24 (or maybe even 32) beats long, so if someone calls an 'Ochenta Complicado' you might have fun by telling your partner you'll just do a normal 'Ochenta', and then throw in some 'mambo' after it while watching what everyone else is doing for 8 beats before returning her to 'Guapea' with a 'Dile Que No' and being ready to wait and swap partners. This way you get to do a bit of the move (the simpler) version, while everyone else does the complicated one, and you're not going to cause any traffic jams.

Los Básicos

When I help a newcomer to Rueda, I teach them five moves – 'Guapea', 'Enchufla', 'Dame'/'Dile Que No', 'Rompela' and 'Al Centro'. I then tell them to just remain in 'Guapea' or 'Al Cento', and watch to swap partners when everyone else does. I think this is important to stress, as it keeps the circle running smoothly, so even with beginners who don't know all the moves (or any!) can still participate and learn.

Here are the moves in brief, just to get you started, with an overall 'philosophy' of each move. I will go into other moves in some detail in separate chapters, but if you are looking for specific, 'step-by-step' instructions on how to learn a move, the best way to learn dance is dancing – if you can, take a class… or if that is not an option, get some friends together and download some videos from YouTube and practice together (see the list in the 'Additional Resources' chapter).

Guapea

Definition: 'Guapo' can mean a handsome, macho man who swaggers or struts around acting tough and usually womanising... so, in this instance, 'Guapea' means to 'man-handle' or control his woman - holding her by the wrist and pulling/pushing her. Try to sort-of *gently* replicate this pushing and pulling feeling in 'Guapea' - a slight 'tap' of the hands on 5 is not really what the move is about... it's more of a connection with an elastic bounce or pushing off of each other and then pulling her back to you again.

This is the most basic move in Rueda, and is normally done while waiting for the caller to call a move. It is important to swing open to face into the circle, as you are dancing with the group as well, not just your partner, but then make sure to look at and smile at your partner as you bring your hands together on 5, before pushing away and open up to the circle again.

Dame / Dile Que No

This is the basic transfer of partners. Guys leads the girl from right to left across in front of him... it is the easiest, quickest way to get women from the right (or 'Al Centro' position) to the left (or 'Guapea' position).

'Dame and 'Dile Que No' can be confusing to beginners. 'Dame' means, "give me one", and 'Dile Que No' means, "tell her no", and they are two separate calls. Therefore, if a 'Dame' is called, you do a 'Dile Que No' move to collect her, without it being called separately. However, a 'Dile Que No' can be called separately at any other time as part of another move.

Note: it is very important in a 'Dile Que No' move for women to wait until beat 5 to cross in front of the man, (leaders, you might have to help make them wait if you can…) so that all the women change places at the same time – otherwise you have two women trying to be in the same space at the same time! I like to think of 'Dile Que No' as "tell her no", meaning that you should 'gently' try and prevent her from crossing in front of you before she is supposed to on beat 5.

Enchufla

Some people say 'Enchufla', some say 'Enchufe'… I have heard it more commonly in Cuba to say 'Enchufe', but you can say either. 'Enchufla' seems to follow a more consistent naming convention of other names, such as 'Rompe_la_', 'Exhibe_la_', 'Vacila_la_', etc. It means to "connect", or "plug in", as in an electrical plug, where the male and female sockets fit into each other. I think it is called this because the male and female dancers kind of come together and 'inter-connect' with each other before 'un-plugging' and changing places.

'Enchufla' is probably the main building block for most Rueda moves. I tell the more advanced beginners, that if they don't know a move, there is about a 75% chance in social Rueda that it is going to start with an 'Enchufla' – so just try an 'Enchufla' and see what happens… if it ends up not being an 'Enchufla' based move, simply hang on to her and do a 'Dile Que No' back to 'Guapea', and wait to watch everyone for when to change.

Rompela

Literally means, "to break", so you are 'breaking' apart the Guapea and changing to 'Al Centro'. It starts with an 'Enchufla', but you hang onto your partner so that you bring her back to 'Al Centro' position. Sometimes you have to think for yourself and use 'Rompela' to do a call. For example, if you have a caller who calls 'Tiempo España' from 'Guapea' position – you will need to do a 'Rompela' first to get into the 'Al Centro' position to be able to do the 'Tiempo España'

Al Centro (also called 'Al Medio')

Starting a Rueda from 'Al Centro' is more traditional than beginning from a 'Guapea', but it can be started from either 'Guapea' or 'Al Centro' position, so watch the caller for his/her preference. If a circle is forming, and I am already doing 'Guapea', and whoever decides to call switches to 'Al Centro', I will simply do a 'Rompela' to get in sync – don't break the beat and just drag the woman across in front of you – make it look classy like you are dancing!

'Al Centro' is a subtle move, of slightly raising your hands up on 1 and lowering them on 5, while keeping steps in place. It is not to be confused with other moves, such as a more dramatic, exaggerated one where you make a 'scoop' down low into the centre of the circle and up again like a teapot spout.

Arriba, Abajo,
Al Centro… Guapea!

For those of you unfamiliar with the common drinking phrase in Central America – 'Arriba/Abajo/Al Centro/Pa Dentro!', which means "Up/Down/To the Centre/To the Inside", I just changed it to include 'Guapea', so that it would be four of the simplest, most common moves in Rueda – 'Arriba', 'Abajo', 'Al Centro' and 'Guapea' – but there is also a move called 'Al Dentro' in Rueda as well!

Now, this chapter is a touchy topic. I am telling you what I have learnt, and what is the normal calling practice in Cuba. However, each caller has their own understanding of 'Arriba' and 'Abajo' and you should watch them to see what they do.

Personally, when I started dancing Rueda, I used to think of the wheel's direction from an aerial overview point - as if I was looking down on the wheel from above... and even more specifically, in terms of clockwise or counter-clockwise movements. I assumed that 'Arriba' meant "up" the wheel, like "upriver", against the current or flow, and therefore 'counter clockwise' – and thus, 'Abajo' was the opposite and 'clockwise'. Then, I realised (...as I should have known in a Latino machismo culture – just kidding! ;) that 'Arriba' and 'Abajo' are relative to whichever way the man is facing at that moment. So, if in 'Guapea' position, 'Arriba' would be clockwise, as the men are facing that direction. However, in 'Al Centro' position 'Arriba' would be counter-clockwise, as the men are now facing 'up river'.

It gets a little hard to understand in practice though, as sometimes a caller will call, 'Dame', 'Dame Dos' and 'Arriba'. Now, you would think that the man is facing counter-clockwise to go collect his second woman, and there for it should be 'Abajo' to go back a partner, but you have to keep in mind that you would actually be in 'Guapea' position (even if just for a moment) when you are supposed to execute the 'Arriba' command and thus you go back, or counter-clockwise one woman. Happily, most of the time it is obvious – as in 'Tiempo España Arriba', 'Ehcufe Arriba', etc.

A Quick Tip For The Partner Leader

In Rueda, a move will usually be called on beat 1, and then begun on the next beat 1. (The hard rule is that you do it on the next possible beat 1 – so that even if a caller calls the move on beat 3 or 5, you still do it on the next 1 beat). The point is that you are always ready to do the move on the next beat 1.

If you miss a call (you don't hear it or can't understand the caller), or if you don't know a call, it is best to just tell your partner "I missed that", "I didn't hear", or if you don't know it, just say "I don't know this one" and wait in 'Guapea' for everyone to finish the move and be ready to swap partners. It is better for you to stay ready on beat to keep the circle going, rather than to try and begin a move late, or not know it and make a mistake and get off beat so that the next woman is left waiting for you to collect her and you have upset the rhythm of the whole circle.

However, if you are an advanced dancer (not an advanced beginner), you can learn to watch the caller and try and do the move at the same time. As mentioned, most simple calls are based on an 'Enchufla' with a variation - for example, 'Principe Bueno', so sometimes if I don't know a call, I just assume it will be an 'Enchufla' with something simple and I get ready to do an 'Enchufla' and quickly watch the caller to see what they are doing. If I can easily follow it, I will try, but if I can't, I will just hold her in 'Guapea', tell her I don't know it and smile :)

'El Cantante'

Calling is more than just knowing all the moves (which you will have to do, as everyone will be watching you if they don't know a move to copy what you do). It is also about feeling the group, and the song. Calling Rueda is like dancing with 50 partners at once - all the things you do with one partner (make sure they have fun, that they feel comfortable with the moves you are trying to do with them, that they are safe and not going to bump into anyone, that the moves are right for the music, etc.) you must now do with 50 partners! You just watch that everyone is completing the moves as called and not bumping into each other because some of them don't know the moves - for example, if you call an 'Ochenta' and a third of the dancers mess it up or don't know it, then you probably cannot call 'Ochenta Complicado', 'Balsero', 'Montaña', 'Sombrero', 'Besito', etc.)

Also, each person will come to Rueda from a different dance school or even another country, where they dance each move slightly different, and more importantly, either automatically change partners after each move or not. I have found the move that causes the most problems with this is 'Ochenta' or 'Sombrero'. I think the best way to make this clear for everyone is to always call each and every 'Dame'. So, if I call an 'Ochenta', I will call 'Dame' halfway through the 'Ochenta' so that everyone knows we are changing partners. If you find you have a group of beginners, or people from different schools who arena bit confused by each other's calling, try playing the 'memory' game described in the "Fun with Rueda" chapter.

Another thing to try and do is match the moves to the song. This can be very easy - if it is a song with a 'mambo' feel, you can do lots of 'Enchufla Con Mambo', or 'Ochenta Con Mambo', and maybe even add a 'Mas Mambo' at the end of it so everyone is stepping into the circle doing mambo. If there is a rumba break in a song, call an 'Enchufla Con Rumba', or "Enchufla Con Reggaeton", etc.

My personal theory on calling Rueda is that it is meant to be a simple folk dance that everyone can participate in and enjoy. I know it can be used as a competition game in Cuba sometimes to find the best dancer, but that is in Cuba, and quite frankly they do it because they can – they are incredible dancers!

It is also sometimes performed as choreography, but again, this is a specialised situation. Most times that people dance Rueda in a club, or in a park, it is a fun, social dance. I like to remember that (as in social dancing) people will have a lot more fun with well executed simple basic moves, than with trying to do complicated moves that nobody knows and sets everyone off beat and cases breaks in the dancing rhythm, so I try and call simple, fun moves that keep the circle moving and people smiling and laughing.

Getting started...

The beat

In most cases, you call a move on the beat 1, and do it on the next beat 1. However, quite often callers will prefer to call on 3, 5 or sometimes even on beat 7 – this is necessary, as in for example, when you want to do a 'Dame', 'Dame Dos, 'Arriba' sequence – you need to call the 'Arriba' before beat 1 (after which everyone will already be starting to settle down into a basic 'Guapea'). Also, some callers just prefer calling on 5 – there is no right and wrong, as long as the dancers have time to get ready to begin the move on the next beat 1, all is good.

Now, just another quick word about the beat - as I've mentioned before, everyone has a different way to 'hear' the beat. It can be from listening to the claves (which can invert), congas, bass line, or even the singer. I personally think that whatever you hear the beat as, is what you should dance to it as. You are the caller and whatever you say/do goes! If anyone says you're wrong, simply reply that you "want to call this song on this beat". Be firm! You will need to be able to 'feel' the beat without thinking about it, as you will have too much else to think about... If they persist, and you don't feel comfortable calling it 'off' your beat, just tell them they can go ahead and call this song on that beat, and you can call the next song.

If when you're calling, enough people get off beat that it is becoming a problem (there will usually be 1-2 people off beat in most large Rueda circles, even if they are just a little ahead or behind the beat) then simply call a 'Foto', and everyone should freeze in some funny photo pose until you start the dancing again on beat 1... I do this by standing with my arm up towards the centre of the circle, like a conductor, and dropping it on the 1 beat when I start dancing 'Guapea' again. This visual clue is a great help to get everyone started on the same beat – sometimes I even just do it a few times while we are doing 'Guapea' to get everyone in sync. Alternatively, if you prefer, as you do 'Guapea', you can simply call 'out' on 1, and 'in' on 5 (or even just call "1, 5" a few times).

What moves to call?

I like to think of the moves in groups. So for example, I have the 'action' moves (like 'Enchufla', 'Festival de Pelotas', etc.) and the 'position' moves (like 'Kentucky', 'Setenta', 'Ochenta', etc.). Additionally, I separate them into 'families' of moves, so that 'Principe Bueno', 'Principe Malo', 'Castigala', 'Castigalo',

'La Policía, and 'La Policía Para Las Mujeres' all belong to one 'family'. This way I can group them together, or alternate them as I wish to keep everyone moving or more sedentary, or to do a few fun, crazy moves and make them laugh more.

It is also important to keep the circle moving, so you should try and alternate the faster 'action' moves with 'the slower 'position' ones. You don't normally want to do just 'action' moves and have everyone running around like crazy! This also helps keeping everyone changing partners. If I see more women than men, I make sure that I call moves that either always change partners at the end of the move, or call a 'Dame' to change partners so that women are not left standing alone for 2-3 moves.

Tip: If I ever can't think of what to call, I simply look at my partner and ask her what her favourite move is and call it.

Another tip: Try not to yell the moves... I had a friend once tell me to lower my voice (melodically) to a deeper pitch and speak more relaxed – it would actually help people hear me better than if I was yelling in a stressed, high-pitched shrill. Somehow, contrary to what you would think, the softer lower frequencies actually project better than the higher louder ones. I compare it talking with business clients – I want to sound confident and 'authoritative', but also relaxed and smooth... think of 'Marvin Gaye' or 'Tom Jones'.

Part II:

Las Figuras

Here are a few basic, fun moves to get you started. There are literally hundreds, if not thousands of Rueda moves if you include all the local variations and made-up calls (I know as I have seen quite a few created just in my Rueda community). I can't even attempt to list them all, nor a detailed explanation of how to do them. If you are looking for instructions on how to do the moves, the best thing is to take a class, or if that is not an option (or the teacher is not teaching the moves you want to learn) try using YouTube videos. There are many great videos, as well as websites, and even apps for the iPhone and Android listed at the end of this book.

Moves From Guapea

Dames!

Dame ("give me")

The most common move in Rueda where guys collect new partner from their right using a 'Dile Que No' (or "just say no") move. 'Dame' literally means, "give me".

Can also be 'Dame Dos' or 'Dame Tres' or even 'Dame Cuatro', where you skip ahead the appropriate number – so 'Dame Dos' means you skip one woman to collect the second woman. 'Dame Tres' you skip to the third follower. I find it really helps to make eye contact with the woman you are going to collect – it gives you time to 'count ahead'... and also lets her know that you are coming for her. It is very important that each leader go in the same direction around the circle to collect their follower. Sometimes if there is a 'Dame Tres' (or even more rare, a 'Dame Cuatro') leaders start going crazy and just running across the inside of the circle to get to their next follower (it is a long way to travel in a very short amount of time!) but they must remember to make their way as quickly as possible around the inner edge of the circle.

Otra ("another")

If someone calls 'Dame' and then 'Otra', it simply means "another", so you would just repeat the last move and do another 'Dame'.

Arriba ("up")

If they call 'Dame', and then 'Arriba', it means to go back one woman. 'Arriba Dos' means to go back two.

Mentira ("lie")

You can also call 'Dame' and 'Mentira', which means "a lie", so that no change of partner takes place, and you return to your original partner. This is fun to do... but only once or twice!

Una Con Dos ("one with two")

Collect the next girl, but clap twice on 7 & 8 before collecting her.

Una Con Tres ("one with three")

Collect the next girl, but clap three times on 7, 8 & 1 before collecting her.

Dos Con Dos ("two with two")

Skip one woman, collect the second girl from you, and clap twice on the way on 7 & 8

Dame Con Manos ("give me one with hands")

There are so many names for this move that I sometimes just call it "El Whoosh!". Basically, it is a very simple 'Dame', but much more fun than a normal one. The guys grab the woman to the right of him by her left wrist with his right hand. Then the leaders 'swing' the followers around in front of them to the left and immediately repeat it with the next woman on the right until the caller calls another move. It is very important to 'catch' the woman you have just swung around in front of you with your left hand on her right arm, to stop her spinning for the next guy...

Dame Con Coca ("give me one with a Coke")

A 'Dame' with a twist! I like to do this one by asking my new partner for her right hand by placing my left hand in front of her as she crosses in front of me. I find I can turn and control her better this way, but technically the move is just turning her by touching her right shoulder with your left hand. Then swapping places with her as she turns, followed by a 'Dile Que No' to get her back to 'Guapea' position.

Dame Con Paseala ("give me one with a walk")

Collect your next partner with a 'Dile Que No', and then bring her back around behind you (swapping hands) and then across in front of you again until she finishes her "walk" in 'Guapea'.

Recoger ("to collect")

This is similar to a 'Dame' but involves simply 'recollecting' your *same* partner if you are doing some move where you and your partner separate. For example, in 'La Policía Para Las Mujeres', you disconnect from her while you pat her down, but then it is implied in the move that you "re-collect" her with a 'Dile Que No'... but if it was not implied, the caller could call 'Recoger' to tell you to re-collect her and return her back to 'Guapea'.

More simple, fun moves…

Caminando ("walking")

The whole group walks 'Abajo' or opposite of the direction the man is facing (remember: 'Arriba' and 'Abajo' are relative to the man's perspective – not the circle's!) so, the circle would be walking counter-clockwise. Basically, the man steps out and around a bit on 1, so he is facing counter-clockwise, and then takes a couple steps counter-clockwise 'pulling' the woman behind him on 2 and 3. Then he returns to 'Guapea' position for 5, 6 and 7, before repeating his turn away from her on 1, and walking again on 2 and 3. This continues until the caller stops it by calling something else.

Echevarría (a surname – maybe actor Emilio Echevarría?)

A fun little foot pattern where you stand in place and 'shuffle' your feet back and forth with toes pointing into the circle.

'Salud A Tu Vecina' ("say 'hi' to your neighbour")

A nice way to "greet your neighbour" with a normal 'Guapea' on 1, 2, 3 and a 'greeting' or hand tap on 5 with the follower on the right hand side of the lead (basically saying hi to the next woman he will collect) and then back to normal 'Guapea' with your original partner. Note: no one moves – it is just a hand tap, or a 'hello' and a smile! :)

Un Secreto ("a secret")

Similar to 'Salud A Tu Vecina', 'Un Secreto' is simply to tell your neighbor a secret. Usually it is the men that loudly 'whisper' a secret into the woman's ear – most guys just make a sound like "pst, pst, pst…"

'(Ni) Pa Ti, (Ni) Pa Mi' ("For you, for me")

There are actually two moves: 'Ni Pa Tin, Ni Pa Mi' and 'Pa Mi, Pa Ti', however they are often confused with each other, as well as have several variations as well, so personally, if I hear any move called with the words 'Pa Ti, Pa Mi', I just assume it will be the simpler move unless your group knows both moves and any of your local variations. It is a very simple move that quite often gets messed up by people clapping in the wrong direction at the wrong time, but it's still fun to do.

Everyone stays put where they are and doesn't move. First, everyone claps in front of themselves. Then they turn to their neighbor (not their partner) and clap both hands with them (like the kids 'pat-a-cake' game). Then clap hands back in front of yourself, and finally clap both hands with your partner. This usually repeats until something else is called, but sometimes the caller will also call 'Bajo', which means "down", and everyone will bend their knees and lower themselves as low as they can until they call 'Arriba' and everyone rises "up" again.

Ping Pong

The simple version is to just stick your bum out towards your nearest neighbor (not your partner) and bump bums with them and then return to 'Guapea'.

'Pa Mi, Pa Ti, Ping Pong!'

You can combine 'Pa Mi, Pa Ti' and 'Ping Pong' and replace the clapping hands with your neighbor and partner with bumping bums!

Un Fly and Un Linea ("a fly ball" and "a line ball")

From baseball terms come two easy, fun moves where you just 'catch' a fly ball by clapping your hands in the air, or a 'line ball' by clapping them down towards the centre of the circle. You can also add 'Dos' to this call and make everyone clap twice, but three times is a bit much!

Yogur ("yogurt")

Basically, just a body roll or pelvis grind. First you jump closer towards your partner, in-between each other's knees and then do a body roll or pelvis grind – be careful not to your knees when jumping towards each other!

Vacilala ("show her off")

This is the place to 'show your girl off to the world' – make a big show of it... Spin her across in front of you and then 'recollect' her and bring her back to 'Guapea' with a 'Dile Que No'. You do not change partners in this move, but a cheeky variation is 'Vacilala Con Dame' where you quickly change partners while she is spinning in front you!

Cadena ("chain")

This is a fun one but takes some care and practice, especially when doing the 'Doble' version. It is quite simple actually, but timing is of the essence. From 'Guapea', everyone in the circle joins hands with the person next to them, and then leaders simply turn their partner on the left in towards the circle and around facing away from them with their left hand (like an 'Enchufla', but in place – no swapping positions). Once this is going smoothly for a few times, the caller might call 'Doble', which means that both partners turn alternately. This is where it gets tricky. I hate to say it, but most leaders are taller than followers, so for the men to also turn, they usually need to kneel down a bit, but at the same time rotate towards the outside of the circle. I find it very important to have very loose arms and grips when doing this move so that you are not twisting anyone's arm or hand. It is also helpful to remember that the guys have to physically turn their bodies to face outside the circle for it to work properly.

The Enchufla Family

Let's get connected!

I have friends from Latin America who see us do Rueda and wonder, "Whoa! What are all these complicated moves you are doing?!" I agree with my friends... I think Rueda is a fun, social street dance that should be simple for everyone to do. I love how you can make a whole dance based on fun variations of 'Enchuflas'!

Anyway, here is a quick break down of some of the many 'Enchufla' based moves you can do. I even invented one once when I had a bad left foot that was numb from sciatic back nerve damage (but it honestly felt fine when I danced... I just could not feel my left foot!) where I called an 'Enchufla' and then hopped on my right leg on 5, 6, 7 to the next partner...

You can invent ANY move you want around an 'Enchufla' – just do something crazy and fun! I just thought off the top of my head right now – if you have a birthday dance, call a 'Happy Birthday Enchufla' and everyone can yell out "Happy Birthday" on 7 and 8!

So, let's connect!

Enchufla ("to connect")

Basic move where the leader turns the follower in front of him and then brings her back behind him to change partners.

Note: Almost every move that either begins, or ends, with an 'Enchufla' includes the automatic changing of partners.

Enchufla Doble ("to connect twice")

Two 'Enchuflas' with one arm stopping the follower from following through on the first 'Enchufla', and then doing a second one.

Enchufla Abrazala ("connect with a hug")

A two-handed 'Enchufla' where leaders 'embrace' the follower before letting her go on the second 'Enchufla'.

Enchufla Sientala ("connect and sit her down")

One 'Enchufla' (using the 'Doble' method of sending the

follower back) and then on the second 'Enchufla', embrace her with two hands and have her briefly sit on your knee.

Note: If the call is just 'Sientala', then you do not do an 'Enchufla' first, followed by 'Sientala' – you simply do a 'Sientala' by itself, and then change partners.

There are many, many moves based on an 'Enchufla' beginning that are quite simple, with just an added little something. For example, 'Enchufla Con Pelota' is an 'Enchufla' with an added clap (usually on 7).

Enchufla Con Pelota ("connect with a clap")

'Enchufla' with one clap (usually on 7)

Enchufla Con Dos ("connect with two")

Two claps (usually on 7 & 8)

Enchufla Con Tres ("connect with three")

Three claps (usually on 7, 8 & 1)

Festival de Pelotas

Basically 3 'Enchuflas' followed by 1, 2 and 3 claps. There is no 'Guapea' in between 'Enchuflas' - it is a fast moving pattern where you do an 'Enchufla', clap, 'Enchufla', clap twice, 'Enchufla', and clap three times in quick succession.

Note: these can also be called individually (as above) to give the same overall effect - 'Enchufla Con Pelota, 'Enchufla Con Dos, 'Enchufla Con Tres' (or possibly simply 'Tres' at this point since most everyone will recognise the pattern that is happening).

Second note: I think it is good manners to clap as high in the air as you can when doing 'Pelotas'... if you clap with your hands out in front of you at face level (where you would normally clap) it is right at ear level right next to the person coming toward you. I have heard from many a woman who told me that the man they just clapped next to nearly deafened them with a loud clap right next to their ears!

Speaking of clapping, here are a couple more complicated, but fun, popular 'clapping' moves...

Nueva York ("New York")

'Enchufla' followed by facing your new partner and clapping once over your head (important: remember her ears!) and then once behind your back (you lower your hands under your bum) and then hopping around for 3 beats before collecting her for a 'Dile Que No'.

Pelota Complicado ("complicated claps")

Similar to 'Nueva York', but more clapping and stomping your feet. I always tell newcomers if they don't know it to just clap and stomp a lot!) Basically, an 'Enchufla' and facing your new partner, stomp, clap, stomp, clap, stomp, clap, clap. Then collect her with a 'Dile Que No'.

Taxi!

'Enchufla' followed by everyone raising their hand and calling for a "Taxi!"

Enchufla Con Bulla ("connect with a shout")

'Enchufla' and everyone yells 'Bulla' ("Booyah")

Principe Bueno ("good Prince")

'Enchufla' with a kiss to her right hand as you pass her

Principe Malo ("bad prince")

'Enchufla' with a (soft!) slap on her right hand as you pass her

Castigala ("to punish her")

'Enchufla' with a slap on her bum as you pass each other

Castigalo ("to punish him")

'Enchufla' with a slap on his bum as you pass each other

Enchufla Con Mambo ("connect with mambo")

'Enchufla' followed by 8 beats of mambo facing your new partner

Enchufla Con Rumba ("connect with rumba")

'Enchufla' followed by 8-16 beats of rumba facing your new partner

Enchufla Con Limbo ("connect with limbo")

'Enchufla' with your existing partner returning past you under your outstretched arms as in a limbo game. Note: your original partner goes under your arms, NOT your new partner – you collect her after she has done the limbo with her old partner.

Enchufla Dile Que No ("connect and tell her no")

Simply an 'Enchufla' immediately followed by a 'Dile Que No' with the same partner – no change of partner in this move.

Enchufla Con Paseala ("to walk her")

'Enchufla' followed by a 'Paseala' ("to walk her") with the same partner, so once more, no change of partners in this move - remember to keep a hand on her so you don't lose her!

Coca Loca ("crazy Coca")

An 'Enchufla' followed by a 'Dame Con Coca' with the same partner – again, no change of partners on this move.

Enchufla Arriba ("connect and go up")

Now, remembering the 'Arriba' is from the male's point of view, an 'Enchufla Arriba' is going to go 'back' one partner. So, you do an 'Enchufla', but do not turn yourself around to advance to collect your next partner in the normal way… instead, keep going 'Arriba, or 'clockwise' and go back one partner and collect her by doing a 'Dile Que No'.

Enchufla Michael Jackson

Another fun one is hard because even though guys go in the 'normal' direction, they must 'moonwalk' backwards two followers. You do an 'Enchufla', but remain facing away from your new partner (do not turn yourself around to collect her) and 'moonwalk' like Michael Jackson past your next partner and collect the second follower. I like to think of it as 'moonwalk' 1,2,3… pause and look at what would have been my normal next partner… then 'moonwalk' 5,6,7 and turn to collect my new 'second' partner with a 'Dile Que No'.

Note: When I am calling this move, I extend my right arm and finger out (like Michael Jackson might have when he was dancing…) pointing in the direction (basically backwards behind myself) that all the leaders in the circle are going to travel, just to help remind everyone so we don't have a pile-up of leaders backing into each other!

La Policía ("the police")

'Enchufla' followed by the leader jumping facing into the centre of the circle after he has brought his partner back behind him, and then she 'pats' him down from behind (checking for drugs and guns) for 8 beats before throwing him to the right to collect his new partner.

La Policía (Para) Mujeres ("police woman")

Similar concept to 'La Policía', but this time the leaders finish the 'Enchufla' by hanging onto the follower (almost as if doing a 'Rompela') and then raising her arms into the air above her head and 'patting her down (guys – watch your hands!) for 8 beats and then re-collecting her in a 'Dile Que No'. Note: you do not collect a new partner in this move, you keep your original follower.

La Rosa ("the rose")

An 'Enchufla' followed by the men entering the circle and backing out raising their hands up from the centre (as if you were picking flowers or roses), and then the women doing the same thing. It repeats until the caller usually calls 'Dame' to collect the next woman on your right.

Note: your original partner should be on your left during the entering and backing out of the circle moves, as you had already done an 'Enchufla' with her and more or less swap positions before beginning the entering/exiting the circle additional move.

Second note: This is a simpler version of 'La 33', which involves the men rotating to the right and weaving through the women who are rotating left. 'La Rosa' does not move – it is just an 'in-and-out' motion without rotating.

Guapo ("handsome")

Similar to 'La Rosa', but just a little more complicated. An 'Enchufla' beginning and then men change hands and hold her left hand with their right hand. Then the men enter the circle and make a low-pitched, male 'grunt' sound, followed by the women entering the circle and making a high-pitched, female sound. Then the men turn the women around towards the circle again after they exit (like the ending of an 'Exhibela') and a 'Dile Que No' to get her back into 'Guapea' position.

Slightly More 'Complicado' Guapea Moves

While none of these moves are technically 'complicado' ones, they are slightly more difficult than the basic moves from 'Guapea'. As I mentioned before… I honestly do not know all the 'complicado' versions of all the moves, and so quite often for example, if a 'Setenta Complicado' is called, I will simply tell my partner I don't know it, and that we will just do a normal 'Setenta', and then wait and watch. I don't suggest this for beginners, but you will know when you are ready to try doing something like this, so you and your partner can at least have a little fun with the normal versions of the moves.

Saborea ("to enjoy")

This is one of my personal favourites. It is like a 'Dame Con Coca', but done outside the circle. So, as you face your partner, you turn your back on the circle so that you are facing out, and you turn her outside the circle, followed by a 'Dile Que No' to bring her back to 'Guapea' position. The only thing that makes this move somewhat more complicated is that it is done facing outside the circle, which confuses some people. It is another one of those moves where you do not change partners.

La Prima / Con Hermana / La Familia

This is probably the most common, well-known move (outside of the 'Enchufla' family) in all of Rueda! It was the first 'real' move I learnt after mastering the 'Enchuflas'. I think everyone who dances Rueda must know it.

It is a move of three separate parts: 'La Prima' ("the cousin"), 'La Hermana' ("the sister") and 'La Familia' ("the family"). Someone told me once that it came about from dancing with your cousin, then dancing with your sister, and then heck, why not dance with the whole family! I love the way Cubans name their moves… or at least the stories we get told about it!

The first move, 'La Prima' is a simple under the arm turn and exchange. This can be called and completed on its own. 'La Prima Con Hermana' is the first move, 'La Prima' followed by an 'Enchufla'. The third move, or 'La Familia' is the first two followed by hooking your arms together and swinging around like a "Dosey Doe" in square dancing (again, confirming my theory that there are really only so two ways to turn a partner and therefore all social dancing has much more in common than we would like to believe). I like to swing my partner around a bit and say "wheee" as we go…

Kentucky ("the chicken")

Another very popular move that is also sometimes called 'El Pollo' (which again, reflects my love of the Cuban tongue-in-cheek way of naming moves… hint: "*Kentucky* Fried Chicken").

Tip: I find it important to keep the woman's hands up on her shoulders or else she might think you are going to do an 'Enchufla Abrazala' or even a 'Sientala' with her instead.

Setenta ("seventy")

There are a couple schools of thought about 'Setenta' – one is that you automatically change after the move since the last part of it is an 'Enchufla'. The other is that you end up having to do a 'Dile Que No' (since you have rotated around so much) and thus end up with her back in 'Guapea' position. Again, the best thing to do is watch the other dancers on this one and see which 'school' they belong to. I personally think it got its name from the 7 shape your arms make when starting the move.

Ochenta (Sombrero) ("eighty", or "a big hat")

This is the same move except that for the 'Sombrero', you bring the arms down before raising them over her head to give the effect of a large 'Sombrero' hat. However, for both versions, there is a difference of opinion as to how and when you bring the woman across in front of you. Some women prefer to be brought across first, and then turned on the spot. Others prefer to turn as they walk across in front of you. Personally, I prefer to bring the women across and then turn them in place as I can feel it gives more stability to their turning. Thus, you are just swapping sides on 1, 2, 3 and then turning her in place on 5, 6, 7. Otherwise, you are making her turning as she walks and it can be very disorientating especially for beginner follower. It also is nearly impossibly o do a proper 'Sombrero' if she is walking while you are turning her - it also looks much better if she is turning in one spot as you raise the 'Sombrero' hat over her head.

Montaña ("mountain")

A lovely move that is often overshadowed by the 'Ochenta' and its many variations and complications. It has a lovely feel of the gentle sweeping mountains and valleys if you do it right.

Dedo ("finger")

The same move as montaña, but one-handed!

Al Centro Moves

Some callers like to start a Rueda from Al Centro position, but remember, when a caller calls 'Arriba' or 'Abajo' (forward or backwards) from 'Al Centro' position, it is from the male's point of view (who could have guessed? ;) so from 'Guapea' position, 'Arriba' means to the left or clockwise around the circle, in 'Al Centro' position, 'Arriba' means to the right or counter- clockwise.

Thus, from 'Al Centro', the first move is usually to begin walking around in a circle – 'Pasa Español' or 'Tiempo España' (the classic closed salsa position with your arms up at shoulder level), with an 'Arriba' or 'Camina Arriba' simply means 'to walk', so you walk forward (or 'Arriba' from the man's perspective). In fact, sometimes they just call 'Vamos Arriba' or even simply, 'Arriba', and everyone knows what it means.

If they call 'Abajo', that would then mean backwards for the men. To do this, on the next beat 1 after it is called, you slightly kneel down on your left leg and gently pull her left arm down (as if you are putting on the brakes) and change direction keeping an eye on everyone around you so you don't have a train crash!

'Tarros' (or 'Tarritos') are where you change partners while still walking either 'Arriba' or 'Abajo'. (In Cuba, to call some a 'Tarro', is like saying that they go with another woman for sex, or cheat on their girlfriend/wife). So, in Rueda, it is the process of exchanging partners, but watch out – tricky callers can call a 'Mentira' (a 'lie') (see below) at the last moment to make you go back to your original partner, so always keep holding hands with your original partner until the last possible moment!

You can also have 'Un', 'Dos' or even 'Tres Tarros', swapping one, two or three partners, either moving forwards if you are 'Arriba', or backwards if you are in 'Abajo' mode.

'Mentira' means "a lie", so 'Un Tarro – Mentira' is a fake, or trick 'Tarro'. If you can understand Spanish, you probably hear this word in a lot of salsa songs (...along with 'mentiroso', which means "liar") by Celia Cruz, Marc Antony, etc.

If it is called and the man is moving forward ('Arriba'), he will keep holding his partner's hand and turn to the left to re-join her instead of going to the next partner. If the man is walking backwards ('Abajo'), the woman will walk around behind him and come back to him.

Un Tarro Con Manos ("swap partners with hands")

The same as a 'Tarro', but you keep holding hands with your original partner while moving ahead to face your next partner. This move can be repeated by calling 'Otra' usually up to 3 times to entwine the dancers together in a very tight, intimate circle. I advise to keep an eye on your partner and her hand during the 'wind-up' so you can give her as much flexibility and arm length as you can to help her – if you keep your arm close to you, it is going to pull her off balance and too far into the middle of the circle.

To get out of it use the 'Carrusel' move where men drop to their knees on beat 1 and the women walk backwards until they reach their original partners. Again, I find it very courteous and helpful to look at your partner while doing this, and if she is new, even gently guide her backwards with your hand so she knows what to do – do not pull her or you might get her off balance and trip over someone and fall into the circle!

Then, as the women near their original partners again (you should know since you are keeping an eye on her) the caller will usually call a 'Dile Que No' or 'Dame', so all the men rise up and collect their partners. Note: you have to listen and watch the caller though, as sometimes they just assume that everyone will do a 'Dile Que No' and don't actually call it. Alternatively, they might wish to continue in 'Tiempo España'.

If we are going to do a 'Dile Que No', I also step back when I do it to give the woman more room to cross in front of me, as we are often very close in a tight circle after the 'Carrusel'. The caller might even call 'Gordo' (fat) first to make the circle bigger first.

Then, if you stay in 'Tiempo España', you can do another fun move called 'Exhibela' (or, more often, an 'Exhibela Doble') which means to "show her off". The man leads the woman to centre and then brings her back again (and repeats for a 'Doble'). It is a fun move that works well once you have made this circle 'Mas Gordo' or "fatter" so there is room for the women to extend their arms out into the centre of the circle. 'Flaco' means to make the circle smaller, or "skinnier".

Turn The Wheel Inside Out

Another trick is to turn the circle inside out. There are several ways to do this, a couple from 'Guapea' and one from Al Centro. To do it from 'Guapea', simply do a 'Dile Que No Doble' or 'Reverso', where you do two 'Dile Que No's with the same partner, so that you end up facing outside the circle in 'Guapea' position.

Another way is 'Por Fuera' ("outside") by turning the follower in her place as the lead turns around to face outside the circle, and then a 'Dile Que No' to get her on the left side so you can do 'Guapea' facing outside the circle. 'Al Dentro' ("inside") is the same move, but brings her back to basic 'Guapea' position facing inside the circle.

The other way is from 'Al Centro' doing 'Tiempo España' and then call 'Sígame', which means "follow me". Start peeling off away from the circle around back onto it so you are kind of folding the line off the circle around and going the opposite direction of the circle, until you are all facing outside of the circle.

From this position, there are several fun moves you can do, such as 'Exhibela Doble' (the women will all extend outside of the circle, rather than inside as normal), and 'Dame Con Coca' is fun too!

Part III:
On Your Own

Your Call!

Are you ready for your first song calling?

Here's a sample 'script' to get your started...

Decide if you want to begin from 'Guapea' or Al Centro
position. I find it's better to begin from 'Guapea', as everyone
can see each other (to help everyone find the beat better), plus
I think it's more fun than 'Al Centro' to do while you are
waiting for everyone – people can mess around and improvise
a bit if they like.

Ok, once everyone is in position and on beat (if people are
talking, don't mind them – if they are doing 'Guapea', they are
ready!) Call a strong, loud, clear 'DAME' to get everyone's

attention that things have started. They should all look at you (or be trying to find you) now that they know who is calling. I keep an eye on everyone to see that they are all listening and have started on time.

Then, I like to do a few small, fun moves to warm everyone up, especially if the song has a quiet, slow intro. I might do 'Salud A Tu Vecina' first. This is a simple move, which is nice to do at the beginning to make everyone smile at each other. But it can be a hard move for people to understand if they don't know what to do, or if they don't speak Spanish.

I know I say not to teach Rueda moves while you are dancing, but sometimes it helps establish a nice 'mood' for the circle, so you can briefly explain a move by saying something like, "Ok, let's say 'hi' to our neighbor", on beats 1-7, and then calling 'Salud A Tu Vecina' on the next 1 beat. So, you only spend one 8-beat phrase explaining in English, and then do it right away. That way everyone has an idea what it is, but you only used up one 8-beat phrase of music to explain it in a way that also adds to the atmosphere of the dance in a nice way (I don't shout at them what to do, or try and teach them... I just 'translate' it into English first as way of an introduction to the move, if I feel it might be necessary).

Another example might be a move one my friends invented called 'Coca Loca' – an 'Enchufla' with a 'Dame Con Coca'. I would simply say; "Ok, this is a new one – an 'Enchufla' and 'Dame Con Coca' – Ready? … 'Coca Loca'!". I describe it for 8 beats, and then call the name on the 1 beat, so everyone knows to start the move then.

You can also add in funny comments, etc. (as I do later with 'La Policía', 'Castigala/lo', etc.) but in general, do not take more than one 8-beat bar of music to do it – nobody wants to listen to you explaining a move, telling a story, flirting with someone, or anything else – they are there to dance! Remember, just like social dancing; do not try and teach on the dance floor – if you can't explain it simply in 8 beats or less without showing everyone, save it for another time... do NOT stop dancing to show everyone a move and then expect them to do it – it breaks the whole mood of the circle.

Then I might do a few 'Pa'mi, Pa'ti's, followed by a 'Fly' and 'Linea'. When the song begins to pick up in pace and starts moving, a 'Taxi', 'Nuevo York' and then maybe jump right into a 'Festival de Pelotas'. However, I try and alternate every quickly advancing "action" move (like an 'Enchufla') with a longer, more complicated "position" move, like a 'Kentucky' or 'Setenta', so that people aren't just running crazy!

All this time I am listening to the music, and if I hear a mambo, rumba or reggaeton break coming up, I will call an 'Enchufla' with whichever rhythm it will be. I also try and match the moves to the 'feel' of the song. For example, if it is "Un Montón de Estrellas", I will go to 'Al Centro' and do more close hold moves to keep it close and intimate... especially in the slow bridges of the song.

If there is another quiet section to the song, or if people are having trouble finding the beat, I will slow things down and do some fun moves like 'Principe Bueno', 'Principe Malo', 'Castigala' and 'Castigalo'... and then maybe even 'La Policía and 'La Policía Para Las Mujeres'.

I find it fun to do all of these close to each other and tell the group something like, "Ok, here's one for the guys – 'La Policía', and if they've been bad, "Ok, girls... now your turn to get even, 'Castigalo'!". Alternatively, maybe "Ok guys, here's your chance, 'Principe Bueno'... and if the girl's liked that, how about 'La Policía Para Las Mujeres'?" You get the idea – mix them up and have fun with them; don't just call the moves, 'work the crowd' and make the group laugh, have fun and enjoy the dance!

If, the music spices up a bit, get back into the more active calls, even simple ones like 'La Prima', 'Prima Con Hermana', and 'La Familia' – all called right after each other, will get people moving. If you really want to give them a workout, try 'Dame', 'Dame Dos', 'Dos Con Dos', 'Michael Jackson', 'Enchufla Arriba', 'Arriba Dos' – people will be panting afterwards!

At this point, to give them a break, I might go to 'Al Centro' position and call some slower, more intimate group moves (especially if the music asks for it). So, call 'Rompela' and a 'Tiempo España – Arriba', to get them walking in a circle. I do a couple 'Tarros', and then 'Un Tarro Mentira', to keep people on their toes! Then, I might call 'Abajo' (remember, it's from the men's perspective, so this will mean going backwards) and maybe a 'Dos Tarros', and an 'Un Tarro Mentira' (remember, this is different if you are going backwards – the woman turns around you this time). Now, I will begin building the 'Carrusel' by calling 'Un Tarro Con Manos'. Once I can see everyone knows what to do, I simply call 'Otra', and 'Otra' again to get three overlaps. At this point you need to be kind of quick, so I immediately call a 'Carrusel' since it takes 8 beats before the men drop and the women begin to walk backwards to return to their partners. I make sure and call what I want to do next early, as I have found most people do a 'Dile Que No', if I don't say anything. I'm happy with that, but will usually call it (or 'Tiempo España') to make sure everyone does the same thing. I would avoid calling anything like an 'Exhibela', as we are too tight in the circle at this point.

Once, back in 'Guapea', it's time to get the circle moving again, so I would do action calls like 'Nueva York', or 'Enchufla Sientala', followed by alternating position calls like 'Setenta', or 'Ochenta' with more action ones.

And finally, it's always nice to try and end the song with a 'Sientala', or something slightly intimate so people are left 'connected', but in a rush, even a 'Foto' pose will do fine!

Now, I know I didn't cover anywhere near all the possible moves you could call, but remember - Rueda is like social salsa; you don't want to force your partner through every move you know, or that you think would look good - you need to 'listen' to her and see which ones she can do, that she looks good doing, and most importantly, that she wants to do. Treat calling a Rueda the same way; listen to your circle (and the music!) and do moves they are capable of and like doing, not just ones that you want to do.

Create Your Own Moves

Combine moves

A lot of really fun moves are created by accident. I know a lot of callers do not speak native Spanish, and it is hard for them to remember the names (or pronounce them properly) so you quite often get mix-ups. One time a friend called 'Setenta Sientala' once, and we all looked a little puzzled – we weren't sure if he meant 'Setenta' or 'Sientala', so we did both! A 'Setenta' followed by a 'Sientala' on the last 'Enchufla' that ends the 'Setenta'. It was a great, new fun move!

Another friend called an 'Enchufla Con Coca' (which would normally be a 'Dame Con Coca') which was a simple mistake, so we all tried an 'Enchufla', followed by a 'Dame Con Coca', and it was great! We named it 'Coca Loca' since it was kinda crazy, plus we were dancing to "Loco Loco" by Miguel

Enriquez, at the time and it matched the music, so we all started chanting 'Coca Loca' in the chorus and a new move was born!

So after you create your new move, give it a crazy, fun Cuban name!

Fun With Rueda

Play some group games

Sometimes after we have been dancing for a few hours and all the regular callers are starting to get tired and need a break, I start playing some of these games to make everyone call.

Alternating callers

Make each woman call a move when they dance with a certain male (usually a more advanced caller who can help them if they don't know any moves). Or vice versa, make all the guys call a move when they are dancing with a certain woman. So, for example, tell your group, "Ok, whoever is dancing with (name of a man/woman) in the (colour?) shirt has to make a call".

Then, of course, as the partners swap, they will all each have to make a call, and if they don't know any moves, they can just call a 'Dame'.

Caller tag

A variation on this is to play 'caller tag' where one person calls a move, and then points to someone else to call the next move, and so on... You can ever extend it a bit so there is not the waiting time between callers by having each person call three moves before 'tagging' the next person.

Alphabet Rueda

You can make the above games a little more challenging by making it so that all the moves called must be in alphabetical order. For example, for the 'alternating callers' game, it would be a simple case of each person calling the next alphabetical move possible (unless the person wants to be a troublemaker and call 'Yogur' right away!).

For the 'caller tag', you could make it a little easier and vary the rules so that each caller has to make their three calls in alphabetical order, otherwise you might run out of calls too quickly!

The memory game

Everyone has to repeat the previous moves a caller has made before doing the next new move called. So, to begin the dance, the caller calls 'Dame' and everyone does a 'Dame'. Next, he/she calls 'Nuevo York', so now everyone must do a 'Dame' followed by 'Nuevo York'. Next, they call 'Festival de Pelotas', and everyone must first do a 'Dame, followed by 'Nuevo York', and then the new move 'Festival de Pelotas', and so on...

This is a good game for groups that do not know many moves, as basically by the end of the song, you are only repeating the same 5-10 moves over and over again, without having to call them repetitiously, so it's more fun to do only a few simple moves this way. However, you can challenge the more advanced groups with longer complicated calls as well, but they won't have to remember as many moves, since the complicated ones can take up to 4-5 times longer to complete each one – you might only need to call 3-5 moves for the whole song!

Rueda de Bachata

Another fun variation is Bachata Rueda. There are many similar moves (even with the same names), but obviously danced to Bachata music using the basic Bachata dance step pattern instead of salsa. I have seen it danced a few times in clubs with a small group of 3-4 couples, or as a choreo performance on stage.

I find it is more of a 'partner dance' than Rueda de Casino (in Cuba, Rueda de Casino is 'Salsa' Rueda) since the moves tend to be longer patterns with the same partner and not as many, (or as quick), partner changes. I think of it more as a slow, peaceful version of Rueda that lets you enjoy dancing with the same partner more, yet while still in a group. I hope it becomes more popular!

Afterword...

I know there will be mistakes, misnames and things I have left out of this book by accident... no book could possibly list all the Rueda moves, their common variations and much less, their local variations. I have tried to just give a taste of the wonderful world of Rueda, how it works so you can understand it and have more fun dancing!

Vamos a Rueda!

More Resources

Schools! Your best bet is to learn Rueda from a school. Google your city name and Rueda and see what you find. If nothing, try asking around at your local salsa clubs – sometimes a salsa social dance night will begin with a free (or paid) salsa lesson – ask them if they also teach Rueda, or if they know anyone who does.

If you can't find a local Rueda class, try creating your own Rueda social dance group to learn moves and practice together. I have organised many of these, using dance studios during the daytime on weekdays, or just dancing in a park or anywhere with a flat, safe surface and preferably some shade if it is sunny.

Books:

"Dancing The Beautiful Wheel", A Guide to Rueda de Casino, by Ian Smith, Cambridge Rueda UK.

Websites and YouTube:

I usually just Google the terms 'Rueda', and the name of the move I am trying to learn to see what is our there... but I have a few favourites that I usually end up having a look at:

"Salsafuerte" has a YouTube Channel in the same name – sort videos by 'most popular' and you will see the best ones

It seems like a lot of the same videos are also available at:

http://www.salsalust.com/

These two wiki lists are quite good for starters...

http://en.wikibooks.org/wiki/Rueda_de_Casino

http://ruedawiki.org/

Apps for iPad/iPhone and Android:

'Salsa Steps' by Papp Zoltan, seems like the only good Cuban salsa and Rueda app available for both Android and Apple. There are quite a few free lessons, and then you pay-per-download for any additional ones you are interested in.

ABOUT THE AUTHOR

Daniel has played drums and percussion in Latin bands since he was 12 and has since directed his musical passion about salsa, son, rumba, timba, mambo, samba, forró and many more rythms into dancing. He now lives in Sydney, Australia, organising free social rueda and salsa dance groups in the parks, helping as many people as he can to get up and dance!

22248876R00049

Printed in Poland
by Amazon Fulfillment
Poland Sp. z o.o., Wrocław